FEMALE FIGURE SKATING LEGENDS

Oksana Baiul

Nicole Bobek

Ekaterina Gordeeva

Nancy Kerrigan

Michelle Kwan

Tara Lipinski

Katarina Witt

Kristi Yamaguchi

CHELSEA HOUSE PUBLISHERS

MICHELLE KWAN

Sam Wellman

CHELSEA HOUSE PUBLISHERS
Philadelphia

CHELSEA HOUSE PUBLISHERS

Designed by Combined Books, Inc.
Conshohocken, Pennsylvania

Cover Illustration by Bonnie Gardner

The Chelsea House World Wide Web site address is
http://www.chelseahouse.com

3 5 7 9 8 6 4

Library of Congress Cataloguing-in-Publication Data

Wellman, Sam.
        Michelle Kwan / Sam Wellman.
            p. cm.—(Female sports stars)
        Includes bibiliographical references (p. 62) and index.
        Summary: Describes the personal life and figure skating
        career of the young Chinese American who won the
        National and World Championships in 1996.
        ISBN 0-7910-4875-6 (hc)
        1. Kwan, Michelle, 1980-   —Juvenile literature. 2. Skaters—
        United States—Biography—Juvenile literature. 3. Women
        skaters—United States—Biography—Juvenile literature.
        [1. Kwan, Michelle, 1980-   . 2. Ice skaters. 3. Chinese
        Americans—Biography. 4. Women—Biography.] I. Title.
        II. Series.
        GV850.K93W45 1997
        796.91'2'092—dc21
        [B]   97-29627
                                                                    CIP
                                                                     AC

CONTENTS

YOUNGEST
OLYMPIC SKATER
EVER?

In January 1994, eighth-grader Michelle Kwan of Torrance, California, found herself in Detroit, Michigan, in the middle of a national scandal.

The commotion started the day before America's National Championships for women's figure skating. Nancy Kerrigan, the skater favored to win, was attacked. After her practice session, a man whacked Kerrigan on the knee with some kind of club and dashed outside the arena to disappear into a squall of snow.

The next day—with the competition about to begin in Joe Louis Arena—everyone wondered if Kerrigan would be able to skate. Much more than the National Championship was at stake in Detroit. America would send

Michelle Kwan skated to the silver medal in the 1994 Nationals after Nancy Kerrigan withdrew due to injuries.

the top two skaters to Norway the following month for the 1994 Olympics.

The Olympics!

Just the thought of that opportunity sent a million butterflies fluttering around inside Michelle Kwan's stomach. Even though she was a 13-year-old who was three inches short of five feet tall and weighed only 79 pounds, Michelle was no spectator. She was a skater herself, who had to compete against Nancy Kerrigan, a medalist in the previous Olympics, and Tonya Harding, a former National Champion and the only American woman ever to land a triple Axel jump in competition.

Even former World Champion Elaine Zayak was going to compete. Harding, the youngest of the three accomplished veterans, was 10 years older than Michelle. And now there was this uproar over the attack on Nancy Kerrigan.

"Why me? Why now? Help me! Help me!" Kerrigan had screamed, writhing in pain after the attack.

Now, just before the competition was to begin, everyone wondered if Nancy Kerrigan would be able to skate. Then the news rocked Joe Louis Arena: Nancy Kerrigan was too injured to compete.

Did Michelle Kwan now dare dream of finishing as high as second in the National Championships and going on to the Olympics? Her coach tried to calm her. But he was excited himself.

Michelle's parents also tried to calm her. But they were excited, too. Every skater, every coach, and every parent in the arena was on edge. Gossip floating around the arena seemed wild to Michelle. Was the man responsible for such a vicious attack on Nancy Kerrigan a crazed Tonya Harding fan, as deranged as the Steffi Graf fan who had attacked tennis star Monica Seles in 1993?

All of America was talking about the attack on Kerrigan. Seven television trucks were now parked outside the arena. A colossal audience was expected for the televised finals—maybe one of the largest in television history.

When Michelle heard that, the butterflies took off again!

She must not let the "little voice" upset her, either. Michelle had heard veteran skaters speak of the inner doubt that gnawed away at their confidence as that insidious little voice. What, chided her little voice, was a wispy kid like her doing here with these world-class skaters? She had not even won a national juniors title. She wasn't even allowed to wear makeup yet. Michelle's little voice sounded like a chorus of obnoxious little voices!

She had to remind herself that she had spent thousands of hours on the ice just as the world-class skaters had. She had sprawled on the ice just as they had sprawled, practicing the same spins and jumps. She, too, had struggled to interpret her music. She also had worried about her costumes. She was just like all the other skaters, she reassured herself.

No 13-year-old American skater has ever gone to the Olympics, her little voice pointed out. Had she forgotten how poorly she always skated in the national finals?

Oh, no! Michelle shuddered.

That really struck a raw nerve; it was so true. Twice, she had embarrassed herself at national finals. She tried to calm herself by remembering her coach's words. That's why she had to practice and practice, he had stressed, so in competition she was skating on automatic. That way she couldn't fail.

Oh no? razzed the little voice. Didn't Nancy Kerrigan fall in the World Championships last year in Prague? Skaters fall all the time, no matter how hard they try not to. Michelle tried to calm herself.

Could she block out so much doubt? There's your hero, Brian Boitano, watching you warm up, noticed the little voice. Brian Boitano? Michelle had seen him jump and dash across the ice to win the Olympic gold medal at Calgary, Canada, in 1988—on TV, of course, because at the time Michelle was seven years old. He's competing in the men's championship here in Detroit, informed the little voice, adding nastily, what are you doing here on the same ice with a 1988 Olympic Champion?

The last taunt made her laugh. Yes, she was a mere molecule floating around among these giants of skating. Why was she taking herself so seriously? Light-hearted now, she patted the Chinese dragon medallion her grandmother had given her for good luck. It hung snugly by her heart under the pale blue costume she wore for the short program. The skirt and sleeves of the costume were dainty and filmy. Her long pony tail was tied with a ribbon of pale blue satin.

Her moment came. Michelle glided out onto the ice. She dashed and jumped and spun on automatic, just as she had in practice hundreds of times, to the pounding rhythm of Khachaturian's "Sabre Dance." Later, for the long program, dressed in cotton-candy pink, she went out on the ice to skate again on automatic, this time to music from *East of Eden* and a ballet by Shostakovich. She skated both the short and long programs without a stumble. Still, the judges had to score on difficulty, artistry, use of all the ice, and many other things besides just not falling down. Then came the impressive scores.

Michelle thought she would explode with joy!

At the end of the competition she felt as if she were gliding in a dream to the victory podium to stand beside the winner, Tonya Harding, and claim second place. Michelle knew a grin split her face in half, but she couldn't help it. She didn't even have her usual fears that her teeth were crooked or that her arms and legs looked like toothpicks. It was all she could do to keep from scream-ing with joy, "I did it! I did it!" A huge silver medal hung around her neck. She had placed second in the National Championships! Didn't this mean she would go on now to the 1994 Olympics in Lillehammer, Norway? At 13, she would be the youngest American skater ever to go to the Olympics.

Michelle Kwan at the age of 13 performs at the 1994 U.S. Figure Skating Championships. She finished in second place.

BITTEN BY THE SKATING BUG

Michelle's earliest memories were bathed in sunshine and sea breezes. She was born Michelle Wing Kwan on July 7, 1980, in Torrance, California. Her father, Danny Kwan, had immigrated to America with his parents in 1971 from Guangdong, a province in the south of China. Four years later, Estella, who would marry Danny, also immigrated from Guangdong. The main city of Guangdong is Guangzhou or Canton, so Michelle's parents and grandparents are Cantonese.

The Kwans were delighted to come to America, but they were proud of being Chinese, too. They opened a Cantonese restaurant in their hometown of Torrance called the Golden Pheasant. The whole family helped at the restaurant at one time or another. Danny also

The years of sacrifice and practice paid off for Michelle as she skated to the gold medal in the 1996 World Figure Skating Championship.

worked for the telephone company as a systems analyst.

Michelle was the baby of the family. Her brother Ron was four years older; her sister Karen was two years older. In 1986, ice skating seemed as distant as another planet to five-year-old Michelle, basking in balmy southern California. It was Ron who introduced Michelle to skating. He was on an ice hockey team. When Michelle first watched him at the Del Amo Mall playing in a game, she couldn't believe it. He moved so fast across the ice! She clutched the rail that surrounded the rink. Skates screeched on ice, spraying crystalline fragments through the air. Padded uniforms thudded together, and sweaty players grunted. Parents and brothers and sisters scattered around the perimeter, yelling encouragement.

Skating on ice is wonderful, thought Michelle.

Estella sat quietly, but her eyes were filled with concern as she watched Ron. Danny Kwan fidgeted and nervously groped for a pack of cigarettes in his shirt pocket, only to remember he couldn't smoke at the rink. When the game was over he was limp. He just smiled when Michelle asked if she could play hockey too. And he just blinked when someone mentioned that ice skating lessons were available at the rink. The two sisters picked up on that right away. Yes, what about skating lessons?

Michelle persisted. It is an old Chinese custom to ask again and again. Or to offer again and again. If a guest came, her grandmother would have to offer tea several times before the guest would finally drink it. So Michelle knew polite refusals were an old Chinese custom.

Michelle soon saw on TV an enchanting

Michelle Kwan's parents, Danny and Estella Kwan, supported their daughter emotionally and financially through years of training and sacrifice. They were there to exult with Michelle when she started winning medals in national and world competitions.

young Chinese-American lady glide over the ice in a dazzling costume. Someone said Tiffany Chin was the best woman figure skater in all of America. Michelle wanted more than ever to take skating lessons. Finally, one Saturday morning, Danny and Estella drove Michelle and Karen to the mall for their first lesson.

Danny just stared when he saw the boots being laced on the feet of his daughters. Michelle was astonished, too. How could she manage such big skates? Someone asked if they had skates with double runners for kids. The woman tying the laces snugly at Michelle's ankles just said NO.

Then Michelle stood. She stumbled awkwardly out of a gate onto the ice, clutching the barrier of boards around the rink. Then she let go and slid across the ice out of control, but coasted to a stop—still standing. Karen was

Michelle was introduced to ice skating at the age of five when her brother joined an ice hockey team. Soon the jumps and spins of figure skating became second nature to the eager young ice skater.

venturing out on the ice, too. Several other children clung to the boards, wide-eyed and wobbly-legged.

For their first lesson, the instructor taught them to scull. Bend your knees, called the instructor, heels together, toes out. Michelle coasted on the ice. Turn your toes in until your feet are together again, yelled the instructor. Michelle felt herself slow down. It wasn't long before Michelle and Karen were moving ahead and stopping when they wanted to. After a while, they were sculling around the ice in large circles. Then they did the same thing backwards. Some of the other students fell again and again. But not Michelle and Karen. Michelle wondered if she was grinning like Karen, whose grin split her tan face ear to ear. Then she noticed the smiles of Danny and Estella were even wider.

Both girls loved their lessons. All week long they talked about what they had done and what was coming next. Ron liked his ice hockey, but his enthusiasm was no match for his sisters' love of skating. The girls soon learned to skate forward and backward without sculling. But they took falls now, too, and they even talked about their falls. They learned to relax, to crumple like rag dolls. That way there was less chance of injury. Week after week, they were either practicing or talking about practicing. They drilled each other: Arch your back, but not too much. Palms down. Hold your hands like graceful flowers. Elbows in.

Their skills improved. The girls begged for their own skates. Each skate blade was grooved with an outside edge and an inside edge. At the front of each blade were a cluster of saw-teeth, called the toe pick. Already the girls talked about blade positions as if they were different kinds of pizza: toe, forward outside, forward inside, back outside, and back inside. They now talked about jumping off the "right back out," rotating one revolution in the air and landing on the right back out. They explained to bewildered listeners that these were the blade positions for the loop jump in figure skating. Of course if the skater used her left toe pick to help the takeoff it was called a toe loop jump. Some listeners asked what happened to the bunny hop. Isn't that the jump small children do on the ice?

Not the Kwan sisters. The girls definitely needed their own skates. At the store, the clerk explained the skate boot needed good stiff leather. The toe had to be protected from the other blade. Also, the heel and instep needed to be stiff or the boot would break down. And most important was stiff leather around the ankle, for support.

The girls needed a good all-around blade with the groove not too deep and not too shallow. Because they were so young and their feet were growing fast, the sales clerk recommended skates that sold for about $50. Several brands of good skates were available for that price: Don Jacksons, Microns, Oberhammers, and Riedells. Of course they also needed proper rink clothing for skating. It had to be warm but loose enough to be comfortable.

At the rink, besides paying for instruction, the sisters also had to buy "ice time" to practice what they learned. The instructor also urged the Kwans to join the USFSA, the United States Figure Skating Association. That would allow the girls to compete and also take the test figures to see just how well they were doing. Danny and Estella realized that if they did everything recommended, the cost for each girl would reach about $1,000 for one year. The cost to the Kwan family was multiplied by two— $2,000!

The Kwans weighed the pros and the cons of this recreation for the girls. It was expensive, but they encouraged their children in activities, as long as they kept up with their homework, did their chores around the home, and helped at the restaurant once in a while.

Besides, the Kwans hoped skating would lead the girls to other activities that would satisfy their artistic temperaments. With skating, they would probably take ballet lessons to learn how to move their bodies with grace and efficiency. They would have the challenge of learning to interpret music, elegant classical music, too. All in all, the Kwans were very pleased that the girls had picked such a refined sport. Soon, the Kwan sisters were fitted with good skates and rink clothing.

It wasn't long before the sisters talked about gathering speed in a "three turn," bending the skate leg for a "left back inside" takeoff, then swinging the free leg forward to get themselves spinning around so they could land on a "right back outside." If the toe pick of the right skate was used to help the takeoff it was called a flip jump in figure skating; if not, it was a Salchow. The girls were more than just talk. Soon, they were performing the jumps they talked about. They began to compete against other novice skaters now, too.

And a very great event for figure skating loomed on the horizon: the 1988 Olympics in Calgary, Canada.

TALENTED, BUT OH, SO YOUNG

With the 1988 Olympics, figure skating seemed to be on TV all the time. First, there was the suspense of who would represent America. Although Tiffany Chin had turned professional and could not compete in the Olympics, there was no lack of exciting female skaters.

Americans Debi Thomas and Caryn Kadavy had won silver and bronze medals at the 1987 World Championships. Jill Trenary had won the 1987 United States Championship. A group of very talented younger competitors included Kristi Yamaguchi, Nancy Kerrigan, and Tonya Harding.

Michelle and Karen watched the televised competition that sent Debi Thomas, Caryn Kadavy, and Jill Trenary to the Olympics. The

Michelle Kwan's Olympic dreams began when she and her sister watched the 1988 Olympics on television. She dreamed of doing her spins and jumps before the Olympic audience.

Olympic competition turned out to be a show-down between Debi Thomas and Katarina Witt of East Germany. They were so close going into the last phase of the competition, the long program, that either one could have won the gold medal.

Just 20 seconds into her four-minute program, Thomas leaped into the air to revolve three times. The triple toe loop jump was magnificent, but she landed on two skates instead of one. "Two-footing" a jump was a serious error. Thomas seemed to give up. Even the young Kwan sisters knew that was a disastrous mistake. No, keep skating! Michelle wanted to yell at her. But the rattled Thomas muffed two more triple jumps. Although she lost to Katarina Witt, she still won the bronze medal.

Jill Trenary was fourth, just missing a medal. What could be worse than that? Maybe not to compete at all. Caryn Kadavy had to withdraw because of an injury.

The sisters watched the men's Olympic competition, too. Sportscasters called it the "Battle of the Brians": Brian Boitano of the United States versus Brian Orser of Canada. The girls knew the compulsory figures counted for 30 percent of the skater's total score. Boitano edged Orser out in the compulsories. The short program of the freestyle skating, which had certain required elements, accounted for 20 percent. Orser edged Boitano out in that phase.

So it all came down to the long program of the freestyle skating. Boitano hit eight triple jumps, including two triple Axels. The triple Axel was so difficult that no woman had yet done one successfully in competition. Boitano won the gold, and Orser won the silver. Michelle's skin tingled when Boitano was presented his gold medal on the podium, with the "Star Spangled Banner" grandly playing and the American flag waving.

I'm going to the Olympics someday, Michelle promised herself.

Michelle loved to jump. She had been captivated by men's skating because the men did such wonderful jumps. In the 1988 Worlds, one month after the Olympics, Kurt Browning of Canada revolved in the air four times to land the first quadruple jump in the history of competitive skating. A quadruple!

Was there no end to the fascination of skating? Michelle studied the subtle differences in the jumps. She learned the order of increasing difficulty for the jumps: the toe loop, the Salchow, the loop, the flip, the Lutz, and the notorious Axel. She wouldn't be happy until she mastered every one of them. Then, she wanted to double them—to triple them!

Although the two sisters talked about skating a lot, both still had the normal interests of girls in grade school. They liked to loaf around in blue jeans. They loved to eat lasagna and pizza. They watched TV. They listened to music. They even played basketball and swam. Michelle liked to collect stamps. So the girls' parents weren't worried that skating had taken over the girls' lives.

Besides, there was the closeness they had with their grandparents, uncles, aunts, and cousins. Having an extended family was an old Chinese tradition. Many Chinese-Americans said "old Chinese," as if it were a thing of the past, but old Chinese ran in the Kwans' veins. There was a vast reservoir of thousands of years of wisdom in the old Chinese ways, including beliefs in the sanctity of family, in hard work, and in managing money wisely. So the Kwans relied on their heritage, as well as welcoming new ideas that were unique to the United States.

One day while the sisters were taking off their skates, the instructor told Danny and Estella that the girls could only develop to a certain level at the mall. The Kwans would have to decide whether they wanted the girls to move above that level or not.

The instructor talked about the Ice Castle International Training Center at Lake Arrowhead, in the San Bernadino Mountains. It sounded remote, but it was only two hours away on the freeway. It was expensive, though, and the girls would need better skates. Really choice skates would cost about $300 a pair and serious skaters needed at least two pairs. They would need finer costumes. Dance lessons. Music lessons. Ice time was more expensive. And, of course, the instruction would cost much more. The coaches at Lake Arrowhead were among the very best in America. All costs could total $5,000 for one skater for one year—times two for the Kwans.

$10,000 a year. It was so much!

The Kwans would have to think a while about that next step. Meanwhile, the sisters labored on their compulsory figures. With all their variations there were many compulsory figures to learn: 70 in all. One example was a serpentine. It was supposed to look like three circles stacked on top of each other. The circles were about 15 feet across. The serpentine was very demanding, with the skater first etching half of the middle circle on the outside edge of the right skate, then switching to the inside

The support of family was paramount in the young life of Michelle, shown here with her grandfather, Ho Yuen Kwan.

edge of the right skate to finish one of the outside circles. Then the skater was to switch to the inside edge of the left skate to finish the other side of the middle circle, then switch to the outside edge of the left skate to completely etch a third circle.

To make it extremely difficult, only two pushoffs were allowed during one complete serpentine. It had to be retraced twice, using the same skate blade positions, a nightmare for skaters. Then, it had to be retraced three more times, switching blade positions and skating in the opposite directions.

How skaters agonized as USFSA officials, sometimes on their hands and knees, scrutinized their tracings for mistakes. How skaters relished it when the Zamboni, the large machine that resurfaces the ice, erased a botched figure!

Was it any wonder skaters dreaded the compulsory figures? Most serious skaters, Michelle had learned, pretended the compulsories were a very good thing—the very heart and soul of skating—while inwardly they hated them. There was a lot of criticism of them in competitions now, especially from spectators.

Many competitions were won by skaters who were masterful in the compulsories but were mediocre in the short and long programs of the freestyle skating. Because most spectators saw only the freestyle skating, they were baffled when the medals were awarded. There was a strong move, especially by American officials, to eliminate the compulsory figures from competition.

One day at the mall rink, while they were trying hard to etch the compulsory figures, Michelle and Karen were overcome by a feeling of silliness. In a flash, they began to play during their ice time. They careened down the ice and tried double toe loops, then double Salchows—anything but the dreaded compulsories. After the girls finished, Danny Kwan walked them to the car in the mall parking lot. He sat behind the steering wheel, tan face tinged with pink. He seemed to want to speak but couldn't. Suddenly he reached into the backseat, grabbed the girls' skates and heaved them out the window. The blades clattered across the concrete.

"The way you skate, don't skate!" he sputtered.

Michelle was horrified. What had they done? Was this the end of their skating?

CLIMBING THE MOUNTAIN

Michelle watched Karen rush to retrieve the skates. When she saw Karen's faint smile, she knew the precious blades were all right. The sisters begged their father not to stop the lessons. One appeal was not enough. After several pleas, they waited nervously. He began to relent. They promised not to goof off like that again. So Danny Kwan kept taking them to the mall. The sisters liked to have fun, but they kept their promise. By the time Michelle was 10, she and Karen had been skating at the mall for more than four years.

One Saturday, Danny and Estella drove the girls up into the San Bernadino Mountains to Lake Arrowhead. The Ice Castle International Training Center was like a fantasy. The rink was walled by mirrors on one side. A skater

Michelle and her sister Karen trained together from a very young age and competed together in the 1995 U.S. National Skating Championship.

could study herself as she whizzed by, or did a spin, or jumped. On the other side of the rink, there was no barrier at all. The ice stopped abruptly against a sitting area. Parents waited there in chairs and sofas by floor-to-ceiling windows that revealed green-pined mountain slopes.

Danny Kwan bought the girls some ice time and told them to practice some routines. While skating, Michelle noticed her parents in the sitting area talking to a slender man. The man had a high smooth forehead topped by wispy gray hair. He would have looked very kind but his jaw was set tight, and his chin was dimpled into a frown. His eyes gleamed intently as he watched Michelle and Karen skate. Afterwards, Danny said the slender man was Frank Carroll. Could he be the same man, wondered the sisters, who coached Christopher Bowman, the skater who was third at the Worlds that year?

Soon Michelle and Karen were being driven several times a week to Lake Arrowhead. Their new coach was the man they had seen: Frank Carroll, the former coach of Chris Bowman. The sisters quickly learned Coach Carroll expected total dedication. They could play around a little but it must never be on the coach's time or during their valuable ice time at the center.

Often, each skater had what was called a "patch" of the rink. Within that patch, the skater had to practice jumps and spins and compulsory figures. Other times, a skater needed the whole rink because one of the things a skater has to learn is to use all of the ice during the freestyle skating routine. Some skaters glide dangerously close to the boards during their dashes and jumps around the ice trying to fulfill the requirement to use the entire rink.

Soon the girls were exercising at the ballet barre, too. Ballet is the ultimate form of body control. They practiced dancers' gestures for basic emotions: excitement, sadness, joy, love, fear, and bravado. They had lessons from choreographers. They learned about the beat and the rhythm of music. They were encouraged to search for musical pieces they personally found appealing so that they might interpret them with great feeling. They were taught to plot their routines on a diagram of the rink.

Rule 323 of *The United States Figure Skating Association Rulebook* was read to them as if it were their constitution:

In the marking of composition and style, the following must be considered:

(a) harmonious composition of the program as a whole and its conformity to the music chosen;

(b) utilization of space;

(c) easy movement and sureness in time to the music;

(d) carriage;

(e) originality;

(f) expression of the character of music.

Remember, the sisters were told, now that the compulsory figures are being phased out, artistry is more important than ever. And yet, the technical portion of freestyle skating could not be ignored either. Judges weighed three factors: difficulty of the program, variety, and the skater's ability. A skater had to master a great variety of elements, including the most difficult jumps. Jumps and spins and turns were expected and it all had to be done cleanly and with apparent ease.

Michelle learned to quickly regain her composure and competitor's drive after falling in competition. She worked long hours year after year to perfect her skating skills.

From their limited competition experience the sisters already knew the scoring system. Yes, 1.0 was bad, 2.0 was poor, 3.0 was average, 4.0 was good, and 5.0 was excellent. But Coach Carroll told them that at the level of skating they aspired to reach, a 5.0 was a disaster.

They had to readjust their thinking. Top skaters received marks ranging from 5.5 to 5.9. It was in that tiny range that wars were waged at the upper levels of skating. Once in a lifetime, a skater might score a 6.0, but judges were very reluctant to give one. A 6.0 meant absolute perfection. Most top-level skaters never received a 6.0.

In late 1990, Coach Carroll startled the girls, especially Karen. She was 12 now, and it was high time she went all out in competition, he said. The national junior championships would be held in early 1991 in Minneapolis, he said matter-of-factly.

Karen and Michelle exchanged amused glances. Weren't there a few hurdles to get over before Minneapolis? First, Karen had to compete in the local competition, the Southwest Pacific Regional. If she was good enough to finish in the top eight, she would be allowed to skate in the regional finals. Then, if she was in the top four, she went on to the Pacific Coast Sectional, consisting of the top four skaters from each of the three regionals. At the sectionals, the top four went on to the National finals, along with four from the Midwest and four from the East. There were many hurdles before Minneapolis!

But Michelle and Karen were about to learn that Coach Carroll didn't think small. He only thought of reaching the top. His every action told Karen she was good enough to reach Minneapolis and any doubts about it were just plain silly. It almost seemed like a dream as he gently prodded Karen through the week-long Southwest Pacific Regional with its dozens of skaters, and then the Pacific Coast Sectional.

Almost before the Kwans could appreciate the moment, Karen was one of the 12 finalists slated for the national Juniors. It seemed worth all the money and time and hard work.

The whole family went to Minneapolis. Naturally, Michelle was not allowed to practice with the Junior finalists. But missing practices was disastrous, insisted Coach Carroll. If a serious skater missed one week of practice, it could take a month or two to regain the same level of competence. Two or three weeks of missed practices was a catastrophe. He shuddered when he said that.

So while Karen practiced in a sumptuous indoor rink that echoed with cheerful excitement, Michelle practiced at the only available ice, a small outdoor rink that whispered only of wintry wind. This was Minnesota, not southern California, she very quickly realized. Skating with an icicle hanging off the end of her nose was not nice, she thought grumpily.

On the way back to California, she seethed. "I'm never doing this again. I'm not coming to just watch."

Coach Carroll was surprised by her outburst. Such a sweet little girl and such a hot little temper. But he did not know the Cantonese temperament. The Cantonese were rebellious people, much more so than the northern Chinese. We're seeing thousands of years of history here, thought Danny and Estella Kwan, with more than a little pride. But just how much of a fire raged inside tiny Michelle?

REBELLION!

The Kwans pondered taking the final leap. Coach Carroll told them their girls had a real gift. How far they went with the gift depended on how hard they all wanted to work. The girls could only reach their maximum potential by living at Lake Arrowhead and practicing several hours a day. The cost would be staggering. For the two of them, about $60,000 a year! Ron would soon be going to college, too. How would Danny and Estella pay the bills? They decided that somehow they would manage. They forged ahead.

The Kwans were comforted by the thought that the girls were getting the very best training. Lake Arrowhead had a great reputation. It was one of a handful of elite centers, the others being referred to simply as Cape Cod, Mon-

Clutching her backpack, "Mr. Bear," Michelle gives an interview at the Ice Castle International Training Center in Lake Arrowhead, California.

sey, Winterhurst, and Delaware in the eastern United States, or Broadmoor in the Rockies, or Costa Mesa in California. "Lake Arrowhead!" a parent from a small center would gasp at a competition. Just being known as a Lake Arrowhead skater got a judge's attention, too. The judge was even more impressed if the skater's coach was Frank Carroll.

Few juniors were as young as 11. But Coach Carroll was relieved when Michelle seemed skilled enough to compete as a junior. She was not a happy spectator.

Then, he began to hint she was more than good enough—she might even be a better skater than Karen. And in the next juniors regional it was Michelle who won the gold medal. But Karen did not begrudge Michelle success; envy of a family member was unthinkable to a Kwan. Michelle slipped to third in the sectional competition but it was still good enough to qualify for the national juniors in Orlando, Florida, in February 1992.

But Michelle grew very tense. Coach Carroll and Danny Kwan tried to help her feel relaxed by minimizing the competition. Again and again, they insisted the other skaters were nothing to worry about. So, even though she knew the national competition was the most important event of her life, Michelle kept telling herself it was nothing—over and over. One morning during the competition, Michelle awoke to find her father distraught. He told her she had been muttering in her sleep, "It's nothing, it's nothing." Tears rolled down his cheeks.

"You are my daughter," he said gently. "Skating has cost a lot of time and money and worry to your parents. But when I see you get too stressed out like this, I think it's time to quit." He paused, and as sincerely as he could, he urged her to just have fun, to enjoy skating.

In the competition, Michelle performed well in her short program, finishing fifth, but faltered so badly in her long program she dropped to ninth. She was very unhappy about the juniors. In fact, she hated the juniors, partly because of the closed judging. For the senior skaters, all judging was done openly by nine judges, as immediately as possible. But in the juniors, the seven judges convened in private after the competition and compared notes. They even were allowed to change their marks after much discussion. The waiting was excruciating for junior competitors, their coaches, and parents. Who knew what negotiations transpired? Who knew if they had lost simply because one judge was more persuasive than another?

Never again, never again, said Michelle.

But this time on the way back to California she kept smiling politely. During the following weeks of practice she asked Coach Carroll if she might not be considered for seniors. He blinked in astonishment and shook his head no. She asked again later. Coach Carroll was not of Chinese heritage. He was perturbed by her persistence. Hadn't he already said no? She asked again a little later. She wasn't ready, he said. Good grief, Michelle was a mere four feet, how many inches? And how much did she weigh? Seventy pounds? She was a good skater, Coach Carroll admitted, better than ninth at the junior nationals. But still, she was in no way ready for seniors!

Michelle thought and thought. The year 1991 had been momentous for figure skating: compulsory figures were being phased out.

Although the compulsory figures had not been eliminated yet for the juniors, seniors no longer had to worry about them. In the past, young skaters had to struggle for years trying to master the compulsories. But no longer. In the senior competition, young jumpers would move up much faster now, some said. They could score very well. Wasn't she a young jumper? Moreover, didn't she just hate the way juniors had to compete?

Never again will I skate in juniors, decided Michelle.

One day, in May 1992, she casually approached her father and asked him to take her to the seniors test that she knew was being conducted by USFSA officials nearby. "Ask Frank," muttered Danny, surprised at her request.

Assured by Michelle that Coach Carroll approved, Danny still wondered why Coach Carroll wasn't taking her himself. He's out of town, shrugged Michelle. Then Danny remembered Coach Carroll was in Canada. Surely Michelle wouldn't ask to take a test Coach Carroll didn't approve of. So Danny took Michelle. The 11-year-old passed the seniors test. Then Michelle took a very deep breath and waited. The most difficult part was yet to come—when her coach found out.

Later she would recall, "I knew I might get into trouble, but I just had to do it."

Coach Carroll had dumped rebels before. Most recently, he had coached Chris Bowman to a gold medal in the Nationals and to silver and bronze in the Worlds. But in 1990, he gave up on Bowman who, without warning, completely scrapped his routine in the Worlds, a routine Carroll had perfected with him for a

year. No, Coach Carroll didn't want another rebel like Bowman. His favorite had been Linda Fratianne. He had coached her to four National championships. She had won Worlds twice. She was the silver medalist in the 1980 Olympics. To Linda, Coach Carroll's word had been law.

"If you told Linda to jump off the roof, she jumped off the roof," he remembered, then said

At 11, Michelle pushed her father and her coach to enter her in the senior competitions—her goal at a very early age was world competition.

of Michelle, "This kid wants a little more input in it. She has respect for me, but I don't scare her."

How did Coach Carroll react to Michelle's decision to take the seniors test? "I was flabbergasted," he recalled later, "that this 11-year-old would go ahead without my blessing. And she wasn't exactly apologetic. She said she wanted to challenge herself against the best. What was I going to do, stand her in the corner for a month? I told her, 'Believe me, little girl, we have our work cut out for us.'"

Coach Carroll gave Michelle a second chance. After a while, she began to wonder if it was worth it. He made her work hard. She was not going to embarrass him. If she wanted to compete against seniors, she would have to train like one. That meant no excuses. If she felt sick when she came to practice, he simply insisted that her illness was a great opportunity. She could pretend it was the Olympics. She had the flu; yet, she had to compete anyway. Usually Michelle overcame her sickness and skated well in spite of it. What would Coach Carroll say if she showed up one morning with a broken leg? He would probably say "Well, we'll have to change your triple loop to a double."

Just how good was Michelle now as a senior? The 1993 regionals were on the horizon. She began to have second thoughts. What had she done? This was not the juniors anymore. Some senior skaters were twice her age. Not only would she embarrass her coach, but she would embarrass her parents. And what about herself? She could almost hear the crowd's remarks: What is that brat doing skating as a senior?

There was hostility toward the youngest

skaters. Michelle knew it but said, "If someone doesn't like me in a competition, I block it out, so that I don't mess up my concentration. I just try to have fun."

Still, Michelle went to her first regional for seniors feeling pretty nervous. . . .

6

NATIONAL FIGURE

Once Michelle started skating to her music she relaxed at the 1993 Southwest Pacific Regional for Seniors. It was pure joy! She jumped and spun and glided around the ice. It seemed so unreal—even as she mounted the podium to receive the gold medal. Her parents looked stunned. Coach Carroll, who was very relieved, assured her she deserved it.

Why shouldn't I win it all? she thought.

Then, in the Pacific Coast Sectional she took gold again. Her parents were shocked. Even Coach Carroll looked surprised. Now she really began to feel as if she were in a dream world. There were only three sectional winners in the entire United States. She was only 12. What had she done?

The national finals loomed ahead. Doubt

Michelle performs during the 1994 World Figure Skating Championships in Japan.

Michelle waves to the crowd after being awarded the gold medal at the Olympic Festival in July 1993.

gnawed at her, and at the Nationals in Phoenix, she sputtered. In both her short and long programs, she ranked sixth. When she watched Nancy Kerrigan, Lisa Ervin, and Tonia Kwiatkowski—all more mature young women—mount the podium, Michelle really could not imagine herself up there with them. Her lack of years now seemed to crush her.

But on the way back to California, she scolded herself. What had she been thinking? Of course she belonged on the victory podium. She would work harder than ever. Next year was the 1994 Olympics. Just the thought of the Olympics made her stomach fill with a million butterflies. There just wasn't anything greater than the Olympics.

So Michelle competed with renewed determination. Coach Carroll took her to a competition in Italy. She won gold. At a competition in San Antonio's Alamodome, a crowd of 25,000 people watched her skate. They stood and cheered her. Michelle threw her hands over her face and cried like a baby. She had won gold in a big, pressure-packed setting!

It didn't seem long before the Nationals rolled around again, but this was even more important than the previous year's competition. The 1994 competition in Detroit would determine which two skaters went to the Olympics. In the midst of the uproar over the terrible assault on Nancy Kerrigan, Michelle finished second to Tonya Harding, leap-frogging past contenders like Elaine Zayak, Nicole Bobek,

Lisa Ervin, and Tonia Kwiatkowski. She had finally relaxed at a national competition and skated her very best. Second place should have qualified her to compete in the 1994 Olympics in Lillehammer, Norway. Michelle would be the youngest American skater ever to go to the Olympics.

But no. The status of injured Nancy Kerrigan was being evaluated. Would Kerrigan be America's second skater, along with Tonya Harding? Or would it be Michelle? Then Michelle got the news. The Olympic Committee had decided to pick Nancy Kerrigan as America's second skater. Michelle was first alternate. Coach Carroll gushed to reporters that a healthy Nancy Kerrigan certainly would have been one of the two top finishers.

Following his example, Michelle said as graciously as she could, "It's a bummer for me, but I was kind of hoping Nancy would be able to go. She deserves it."

But what did first alternate mean? Usually being first alternate was about as valuable as Monopoly money, but this was no ordinary Olympics. First of all, Nancy Kerrigan might not recuperate enough to compete. Second, there were rumors that Tonya Harding might be involved in the assault. If that was proven, she would not be allowed to compete. Soon it came out that the masterminds behind the attack were Harding's bodyguard and her ex-husband. It seemed the entire nation was debating what to do about Tonya Harding—even the President of the United States. The opinion prevailed that, unless Harding was charged with a crime, she should be allowed to skate.

In February, just 10 days before the women's competition began, Michelle flew to

Norway with the team and trained. Would she skate or not? Day after day she wondered. Nancy Kerrigan seemed healthy again, but what about Tonya Harding? Harding arrived several days later, seemingly out of shape, and forgetting to bring some of her equipment. In practice, she missed jumps and rarely completed any of her routines. But Michelle knew how distracting public attention was. Harding must have been exposed to a thousand times what Michelle had ever endured.

When the competition began, it was Tonya Harding skating for America, not Michelle. Harding floundered, finishing far back in the pack. On the other hand, Kerrigan was flawless. Never had she skated so well. She easily won the short program. Oksana Baiul, a 16-year-old Russian, was a distant second. In her long program, Kerrigan hit five triple jumps, including an extremely difficult triple-triple combination. Combinations dazzled judges because the second jump demanded enormous effort coming immediately after the first. Yet Kerrigan lost the gold medal to young Baiul. What had happened? Baiul won the long program only with a tiebreaker. But the long program counted twice as much as the short program.

Figure skating did not drop out of the public eye after the Olympics. The dark side of skating intrigued America. Tonya Harding pleaded guilty to hindering the investigation of the attack on Kerrigan, and the USFSA banned her from amateur skating. Kerrigan herself turned professional. Television producers discovered America could not get enough skating on TV. Even amateurs, called eligibles among skaters, began to make a lot of money. Michelle and

*Michelle skates in the
1995 Nationals to a silver
medal. Her coach felt her
little girl image had hin-
dered her finishing with
the gold.*

Karen were held back though. They still had
much to learn in their training.

With both Kerrigan and Harding out of the
eligible ranks, many were saying Michelle was
the next star. She was interviewed by newspa-
per reporters, and she appeared on TV. She was
pictured and quoted in national magazines like
People, Newsweek, Time, Sports Illustrated, and
Seventeen. Strangers now asked for her auto-
graph. They fawned over her. They knew all

Michelle, shown here skating in the 1995 World Championships, impressed many with her drive and hard work— including champion skater Brian Boitano, who worked with her in his spare time.

about the Chinese dragon medallion she wore for good luck. They knew all about the fortune cookie prediction she had pasted in her scrapbook: "You are entering a time of great promise and overdue rewards." Her life was taking off!

Everyone expected Michelle to win the 1995 Nationals. But the older, more experienced Nicole Bobek unexpectedly focused her efforts and won the Nationals, then took bronze in the Worlds. Michelle was right behind her, second at Nationals and fourth at Worlds. Karen had excelled too, finishing fifth at Nationals. But in Coach Carroll's mind, Michelle should have finished higher. She had learned to relax and skate her best under pressure. He heard remarks about her pony tail and lack of makeup. Her little girl look rubbed many of the judges the wrong way. Michelle had to change her image.

Coach Carroll's obstacle was Michelle's parents. To them a 14-year-old was too young to wear makeup. Recalling the confrontation, Carroll said, "I had to say, 'If you're appearing in the ballet, you have to look the part. There's nothing extraordinary about wearing makeup. . . . We're not taking school exams, we're performing in front of thousands of people.'"

Finally, Danny and Estella relented. Yes, they had to admit, Michelle's performances on ice were like those of a dancer on the stage. Dancers wear heavy makeup to make sure they are seen and appreciated by the audience. They allowed Coach Carroll and choreographer Lori Nichol to work on a new identity for Michelle on the ice.

Meanwhile, Michelle toured with Brian Boitano. According to Carroll, "Great skating breeds great skating." Nothing pleased Coach Carroll more than to hear that Boitano was so impressed by Michelle's hard work that he had taken to coaching her himself in his spare time. When Michelle wasn't touring, she lived and trained at Lake Arrowhead, with Karen. Since Ron had gone to college, Estella left Torrance to live at Lake Arrowhead, too. Their cabin was dubbed Debi Thomas' Tee Pee. Other cabins were called Sonja Henie's Hideaway and Brian Boitano's Bungalow, all named after famous skaters. Danny took early retirement from the phone company but lived in Torrance and helped at the Golden Pheasant. He commuted to Lake Arrowhead several times a week.

As the 1996 Nationals approached, Michelle had more than an image problem. Since the 1994 Nationals, she had shot up five inches and gained 21 pounds. She was now a more curvaceous, more statuesque, 5 feet 2 inches tall and 100 pounds, but every extra inch and every extra pound made Coach Carroll cringe. Besides having an image problem, was the maturing Michelle losing her athleticism?

INTERNATIONAL STAR

$\mathbf{A}$t the 1996 Nationals in San Jose, Michelle took on her image problem first. Coach Carroll later laughed about Michelle's arrival there. "I knew it would work before she even took the ice when I heard people saying, 'Who is that girl with Frank?'"

Michelle's floppy pony tail was gone. Now, her hair was woven into a tight chignon at the back of her head. Her makeup was bright and exotic. Her nails were painted. Michelle's new costumes and routines were a radical change too. No longer was she the young thing jumping frenetically to "Saber Dance." Now she was a temptress. Her costumes were rich and trimmed in gold, mostly in shades of rose and burgundy, which suggested exotic Eastern locales. She skated to "Romanza" and

Michelle Kwan smiles after finishing her gold medal performance in the free skating program at the 1996 U.S. National competition.

Michelle jubilantly waves her flowers on the awards platform at the 1996 U.S. National Championships.

"Salome's Dance." Lori Nichol's choreography was a showcase for Michelle's artistry.

Michelle psyched herself up, insisting that in years past she "didn't even know what artistic was." But had the more mature Michelle lost her athleticism? For her long program of "Salome" she began with a triple Lutz–double toe loop combination, followed by a triple toe loop–triple toe loop combination, culminating in a camel spin. Next she hit a triple flip, then a double Axel, before performing a layback spin. These were followed by a triple loop, a triple Salchow, a combination spin, a triple Lutz, a sit spin, and a double Axel. She had mastered every element of skating except the notorious triple Axel, but no current American woman was doing the triple Axel.

Michelle's programs had advanced even beyond artistry and athleticism. Her routine was a seamless blend of all elements. Her victory in the 1996 Nationals seemed almost too easy. She received first place marks from all nine judges. The *New York Times* of January 22, 1996, said she "displayed power, elegance and a new-found maturity." But Michelle knew the Worlds would not be so easy. There she would face a legion of world-class skaters, including Midoro Ito, one of only two women ever to complete a triple Axel, and the most formidable skater of all, defending World Champion Chen Lu of China.

In the short program Ito tried her famous triple Axel and fell sprawling. There is an axiom in skating: a gold medal cannot be won in the short program but it can be lost. Ito had definitely lost the gold. Michelle skated flawlessly. So did Chen Lu. Michelle got the best marks from the judges. Yet, Michelle remembered clearly that Nancy Kerrigan had won the short program in the 1994 Olympics but lost the gold anyway. On the day of the long program, Michelle waited nervously to skate. She hated to skate last. The wait seemed like it took forever.

But on this day, waiting to skate became a nightmare.

Michelle and Coach Carroll were in the flower girls' room where they could not be disturbed. Chen Lu was skating. Thunderous applause erupted. Michelle already knew Chen Lu had planned six triples, including two in combination. She must have hit every one of them. Then the announcement of the scores boomed over the audio system. For artistry, Chen Lu received two 6.0's!

Michelle thought, "Oh god, I'll have to do a quadruple toe loop to win."

Coach Carroll later remembered, "I had about two seconds to say something intelligent and meaningful before she had to go out and skate. So I told her those were fabulous marks, but the judges had left room for her to win."

Michelle bolstered herself, "Just go for it. Go for everything. Why not?" By the time she started

Her new more mature, more sophisticated image helped Michelle impress the judges in the 1996 skating competitions. Here she skates in the Grand Prix in Paris.

skating, she was on fire. "Nothing could stop me," she recalled. "If a brick wall had been on the ice, I would have just rammed right through it."

Even with that determination she got off to a shaky start. She didn't build up enough speed for her combination triple toe loop–triple toe loop. She had to reduce the second toe loop to a double. But it was not an error. After that, she skated without blemish. Near the end of the program was a planned double Axel. After reneging on her triple-triple combination Michelle was sure she needed more than a double Axel. She launched a toe loop, revolved three times and landed perfectly. With that triple toe loop—her seventh triple jump—she brought her program to a close, awash in applause. Hands over her face, she sobbed with joy.

"The emotions took over when I realized this was the world championships and I'd just skated the best I ever had in my life," she said afterwards.

For artistry the judges gave Michelle two 6.0s and seven 5.9s. She edged out Chen Lu for the World Championship! The president of the USFSA was as awed as everyone else, "I never saw two performances like that in my life. For Michelle to add that jump in the last seconds, that's sport."

Coach Carroll was bursting with pride. "Michelle is tough as nails."

Few knew that Michelle slept with her gold medal for the next several months. Life was hectic for Michelle now. As an eligible, she was allowed to join the Campbell's Soup Tour, where she would likely make $1 million before the next Nationals competition in 1997. And she was interviewed endlessly.

Meanwhile, she had to try to keep up with

her high school studies, and she was trying to decide which college to attend. Harvard was high on her list. Karen was already in Massachusetts at Boston University. In competitions, Michelle remained unbeatable. She even beat Kristi Yamaguchi, the professional many skating experts considered the best woman skater in the world. Michelle's accomplishments seemed superhuman. By late 1996, she had been given a spot in every competition in the immediate future, including the 1998 Olympics.

Michelle began thinking of a great future. To the *New York Times* she rashly admitted, "I want to be a legend, like Dorothy Hamill and Peggy Fleming. Janet Lynn didn't win an Olympic title, but in every skater's mind she's a legend. I want to leave a little mark: 'Michelle Kwan was a great skater, artistically and technically. She had the whole package.' I want people to remember me after 1,000 years when skating is weird and people are doing quintuple jumps."

Danny Kwan squirmed at such unbridled optimism. "Don't start thinking you're special. The trouble begins when you start building a wall around you."

And had Michelle read comments made about her by Lisa Ervin? A fallen star at only 17, Ervin warned, "Everything's peachy keen (when you're that young) and the only thing you're worried about is how many double Axels am I going to do today? I remember that. I really feel for her. She's going to wake up at 15 or 16 and she's going to say to herself, 'Oh my god, I'm number one or number two in the nation, and once you hit number one, there's no place to go but down."

Would Lisa Ervin's grim prophesy come true?

8

COMING BACK AT 17

In the 1997 Nationals at Nashville, after winning the short program, Michelle may have suddenly started hearing the inner doubts that Lisa Ervin predicted. Skating to a Taj Mahal theme for her long program, she successfully hit her triple Lutz–double toe loop combination. She immediately launched a triple toe loop–triple toe loop. Seven triples and two combinations in a row were what made her so unbeatable.

But this time she fell on the second triple toe. She sprawled on the ice! She was stunned. This could not be happening. Soon after that she stumbled at the end of a triple flip. Then she fell on a triple loop. Her long program was a catastrophe. Michelle felt lucky to get the silver medal. Tara Lipinski, 4 feet 8 inches tall

Michelle won the short program at the 1997 U.S. Nationals but would fall to a disappointing second place behind Tara Lipinski after the long program.

Her poor performance in the 1997 Nationals stunned Michelle, shown here performing a graceful turn in the short program.

and 75 pounds, won the gold. At 14, Lipinski was the youngest American champion ever.

Michelle seemed like she was in a coma. Had she been too tense? Or had she been overconfident? Should she have cut her second triple toe back to a double as she had done in the 1996 Worlds? She tried to get herself together before the 1997 Worlds in Switzerland. Once there, however, life continued to spin out of control for Michelle. First, her friend and fellow skater Scott Hamilton revealed he had cancer. Then, Nicole Bobek's renowned coach Carlo Fassi, the mentor of Dorothy Hamill and Peggy Fleming, died after a massive heart attack.

Michelle's skating in the Worlds was even shakier than in the Nationals. This time, she missed a triple Lutz jump in the short program. She remembered the axiom; yes, surely she had already lost the championship by flubbing her short program. Coach Carroll recalled, "In the car on the way back from the arena after the short program, Michelle was very angry, in tears, saying terrible things about how stupid she was to miss that jump. Suddenly she stopped short. 'Why am I doing this to myself?' she said. 'Scott Hamilton's fighting for his life.' She realized that winning this world championship wasn't life or death. She used to see Carlo at the rink every day. I reminded her of that conversation before she went out for her long program."

Michelle redeemed herself and finished first in the long program. Had she been second in the short program, she probably would have won the Worlds gold, but she had been fourth. Again, Tara Lipinski won the gold and Michelle won the silver. But Michelle was pleased; she had gotten herself back on track. "Today I got my act back together," she said. "I told myself, 'We have to put this in perspective. Let's just go out and have fun.'"

She let this new-found philosophy work for her at the 1998 U.S. Nationals in Philadelphia. Michelle's performances were practically flawless; she regained the U.S. National title, beating Lipinski, who took second place.

Michelle's win guaranteed her a spot on the Olympic team for the games in Nagano, Japan, where again she skated cleanly and was in first place entering the free skate. But Tara was right

Michelle was back on track at the 1997 World Championship, coming in first in the long competition and winning the silver medal.

behind, and after Michelle had a slight bobble on a triple flip jump, Lipinski won the gold. Michelle settled for the silver. Still, Kwan insisted, "I didn't lose the gold, I won the silver." Now Michelle Kwan has her sights set on gold at the Games in 2002!

CHRONOLOGY

1980   Michelle Wing Kwan born on July 7 in Torrance, California, youngest of three children of parents who immigrated from China.

1986   Along with sister Karen, sees brother Ron play ice hockey at local mall and is completely smitten by ice skating.

1987   First competes in figure skating at age 7.

1988   Sees Brian Boitano win Olympic gold. Winning a gold medal becomes her greatest goal.

1990   Begins training with Karen at Lake Arrowhead, California, under world-class coach Frank Carroll.

1991   Watches as Karen competes in National juniors at Minneapolis.

1992   Ninth at National juniors but hates secret judging. Angers coach by taking the seniors test against his wishes.

1993   Sixth at senior Nationals—at the age of 12.

1994   Second at senior Nationals, but is bumped off Olympic team by return of injured Nancy Kerrigan. Goes to Norway as the first alternate but doesn't compete.

1995   Second at Nationals, fourth at World Championships. Coach says she must dress and look older to get votes from judges.

1996   Stuns skating world dressed in a costume as exotic temptress, wins National and World Championships. On tour, makes $1 million.

1997   Places second in the U.S. National Figure Skating Championship and World Figure Skating Championship.

1998   Regains National and World Championship titles. Wins silver medal at the Winter Olympics in Nagano, Japan.

1999   Wins National Championship title, but takes silver in World Championships after an illness. Announces intention to attend UCLA in fall.

SUGGESTIONS FOR FURTHER READING

Brennan, Christine. *Inside Edge*. New York: Scribner, 1996.

Brownstone, David M.. *The Chinese-American Heritage*. New York: Facts on File, 1988.

Chen, Jack. *The Chinese of America*. San Francisco: Harper & Row, 1980.

Coffey, Frank and Filip Bondy. *Dreams of Gold: The Nancy Kerrigan Story*. New York: St. Martin's Paperbacks, 1994.

Coffey, Frank and Joe Layden. *Thin Ice: The Complete Uncensored Story of Tonya Harding*. New York: Pinnacle Publishing, 1994.

Fassi, Carlo. *Figure Skating with Carlo Fassi*. New York: Charles Scribner's Sons, 1980.

Gutman, Dan. *Ice Skating: From Axels To Zambonis*. New York: Viking, 1995.

Hagan, Patricia, editor. *Spalding Figure Skating: Sharpen Your Skills*. Indianapolis: Masters Press, 1995.

Harris, Ricky. *Choreography and Style for Ice Skaters*. New York: St. Martin's Press, 1980.

Heller, Mark, editor. *The Illustrated Encyclopedia of Ice Skating*. New York: Paddington Press Ltd., 1979.

Olgilvie, Robert. *Basic Ice Skating Skills: An Official Handbook Prepared for The United States Figure Skating Association*. Philadelphia: J. B. Lippincott, 1968.

Petkevich, John Misha. *The Skater's Handbook*. New York: Charles Scribner's Sons, 1984.

Petkevich, John Misha. *Sports Illustrated Figure Skating: Championship Techniques*. New York: Winner's Circle Books, 1989.

ABOUT THE AUTHOR

Sam Wellman lives in Kansas. He has college degrees from the Midwest and the Ivy League. He is the author of a number of biographies about a diverse group of notable people, including Billy Graham and Christopher Columbus. He writes both for adults and younger readers.

INDEX

PICTURE CREDITS
AP/Wide World Photos: 2, 11, 12, 15, 16, 20, 25, 28, 31, 34, 39, 44, 48, 50, 52, 53, 56, 58, 60;
photo © J. Barry Mittan: 6, 47.